Damage Noted:
rec'd w/ slight water damage to top
Date 26 May. '17   JF   BRIT 212

Pebble™ Plus

Bugs, Bugs, Bugs!

Flies

by Margaret Hall

Consulting Editor: Gail Saunders-Smith, PhD
Consultant: Laura Jesse, Extension Associate
Department of Entomology
Iowa State University
Ames, Iowa

Capstone press

Mankato, Minnesota

Pebble Plus is published by Capstone Press,
151 Good Counsel Drive, P.O. Box 669, Mankato, Minnesota 56002.
www.capstonepress.com

1 2 3 4 5 6 11 10 09 08 07 06

Library of Congress Cataloging-in-Publication Data
Hall, Margaret, 1947–
    Flies / by Margaret Hall.
    p. cm.—(Bugs, bugs, bugs!)
    Summary: "Simple text and photographs present flies, how they look, and what they do"—Provided
by publisher.
    Includes bibliographical references and index.
    ISBN-13: 978-0-7368-5350-7 (hardcover)
    ISBN-10: 0-7368-5350-2 (hardcover)
    1. Flies—Juvenile literature. I. Title. II. Series: Pebble plus. Bugs, bugs, bugs!
QL533.2.H35 2006
595.77—dc22   2005023787

Editorial Credits
Mari C. Schuh, editor; Linda Clavel, set designer; Kia Adams, book designer; Jo Miller, photo researcher;
    Scott Thoms, photo editor

Photo Credits
Bill Johnson, 6–7
Digital Vision Ltd., back cover
Dwight R. Kuhn, 13
NHPA/Stephen Dalton, 18–19
Pete Carmichael, cover, 1, 11, 15, 16–17
Rob Curtis, 5, 8–9
Visuals Unlimited/Michael Durham, 21

Note to Parents and Teachers

The Bugs, Bugs, Bugs! set supports national science standards related to the diversity of life and heredity. This book describes and illustrates flies. The images support early readers in understanding the text. The repetition of words and phrases helps early readers learn new words. This book also introduces early readers to subject-specific vocabulary words, which are defined in the Glossary section. Early readers may need assistance to read some words and to use the Table of Contents, Glossary, Read More, Internet Sites, and Index sections of the book.

Table of Contents

What Are Flies?

Flies are insects
with two wings
and six legs.

5

How Flies Look

Flies can be many colors.

Most flies are brown,

black, or gray.

Some flies are smaller
than a person's fingernail.
Other flies can be as
large as a paper clip.

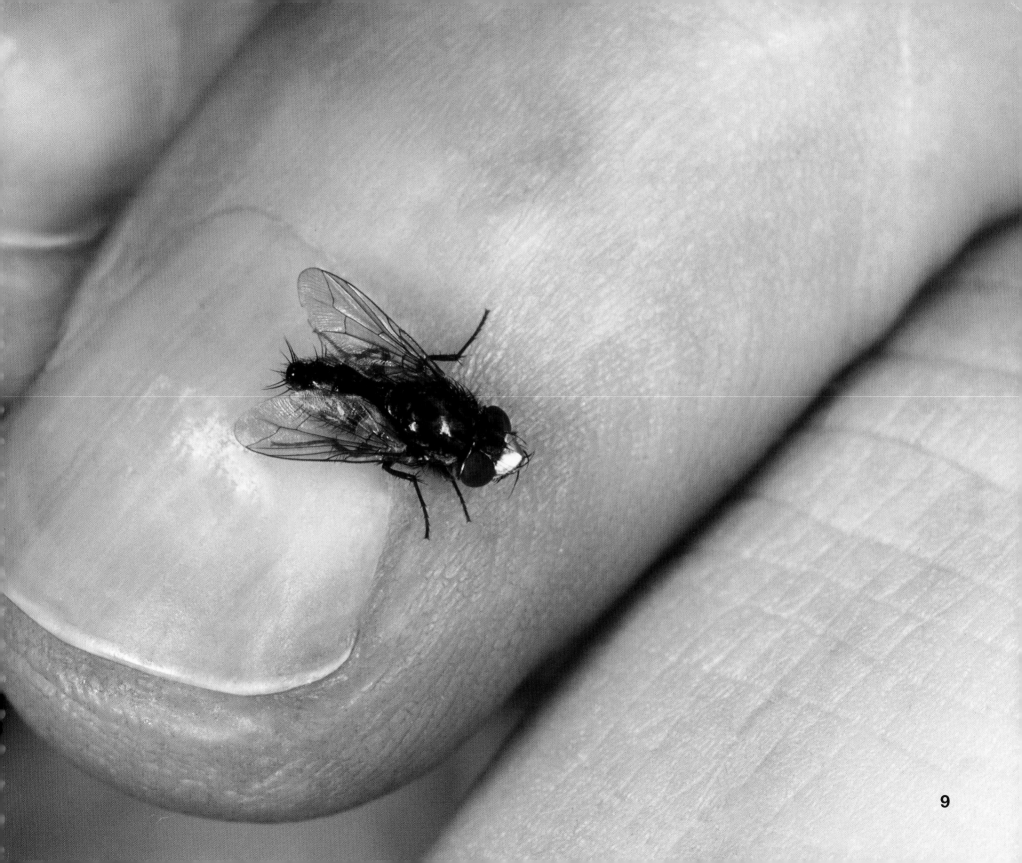

Flies have two big eyes.

Each eye has

many small lenses.

Flies can see very well.

What Flies Do

Flies walk upside down
with their sticky feet.

Flies suck nectar
from plants.
Flies carry pollen
from plant to plant.

Some female flies bite
people and animals.
They need a meal
before making eggs.
Blood helps them make eggs.

Female flies lay eggs.

The eggs hatch into larvas.

The larvas quickly grow

into pupas.

The pupas become flies
with strong wings.
The flies zoom away.

Glossary

female—an animal that can give birth to young animals or lay eggs

insect—a small animal with six legs, three body sections, and two antennas; most insects have wings and can fly.

larva—a fly in the second stage of life; a larva hatches from an egg; larvas often look like worms.

nectar—a sweet liquid that flies and other insects gather from flowers

pollen—tiny, yellow grains in flowers

pupa—a fly in the third stage of life; a pupa becomes an adult fly.

wing—a movable part of an insect or a bird that helps it fly; most insects have four wings, but flies have two wings.

Read More

McEvey, Shane F. *Flies.* Insects and Spiders. Philadelphia: Chelsea House, 2001.

Morgan, Sally. *Flies and Mosquitoes.* Looking at Minibeasts. North Mankato, Minn.: Thameside Press, 2001.

Richardson, Adele. *Insects.* Exploring the Animal Kingdom. Mankato, Minn.: Capstone Press, 2005.

Internet Sites

FactHound offers a safe, fun way to find Internet sites related to this book. All of the sites on FactHound have been researched by our staff.

Here's how:

1. Visit *www.facthound.com*

2. Type in this special code **0736853502** for age-appropriate sites. Or enter a search word related to this book for a more general search.

3. Click on the **Fetch It** button.

FactHound will fetch the best sites for you!

Index

Word Count: 120
Grade: 1
Early-Intervention Level: 13